insulted

humiliated

betrayed

angry

left out

let down

grumpy

frustrated

irritated

worried

content

annoyed

cared for

calm

heard

important

open

The Grump Meter: A Family Tool for Anger Control
Copyright © 2011 Janet Kaufman, Ph.D., Lynn Kaufman, MSW
www.grumpmeter.com

Library of Congress Cataloging-in-Publication Data is available.
ISBN: 978-0-615-54406-9

Janet Kaufman Ph.D., Lynn Kaufman, MSW
The Grump Meter: A Family Tool for Anger Control

Summary: The Grump Meter is a tool for children and teens, families, teachers and mental health professionals to learn how to manage anger, prevent temper tantrums, and avert destructive and self-destructive behavior. The book offers practical, tangible approaches for talking with young people about anger, helping them recognize oncoming anger signs and equipping them with skills to take control of their behavior.

1. Anger – Children and Families
2. Mood Changes – Teens and Children
3. Temper Tantrums – Parenting

Illustrations by Rachel Kaufman and Jonah Kaufman
Graphic Design by David Kreitzer

the grump meter ™

Lynn Kaufman, MSW & Janet Kaufman, Ph.D.

Illustrations by Rachel & Jonah Kaufman

TABLE OF CONTENTS

A PREFACE FOR PARENTS AND OTHER GROWNUPS

You wouldn't think that a colored piece of cardboard could make such a difference in kids' lives. Transformed into the Grump Meter, that piece of cardboard is the subject of this book. Blue is calm, green is grumpy, yellow is caution like a yellow traffic light, and orange is your last chance to stop before rising to red—explosive, destructive, and self-destructive anger.

The Grump Meter is a tool for everyone in the family. It's not complicated and doesn't take a long time to learn. You can begin using it right away. It is for children and teens, from 3 year olds to 18 year olds. Young people identified as having severe mood and behavior disorders use the Grump Meter, and children and parents use it in what you might call run-of-the-mill situations: young children with temper tantrums, and older children and teens with disruptive anger or outbursts. Parents have found the Grump Meter effective for themselves as well as their children.

We have seen children and teens, no matter how complicated they appear or how disruptive they can be, learn to prevent out-of-control and dangerous outbursts, prevent the creation of bad memories, and find more peaceful ways of being in the world.

The book has two parts. The first part is for families to read together. It introduces the five colors of the Grump Meter and the main goal of using it: to learn the ability to calm down and prevent the rise to red—to prevent behavior that is explosive or destructive to oneself or others.

The second part of the book, intended for adults, offers more extensive ideas about how to use the Grump Meter in families, some insight into our thinking about it, models of conversations to have with children about their own emotional regulation, and kids' own words about the Grump Meter.

The book invites you to have fun. Enjoy the coloring. Enjoy learning about each other. Enjoy new conversation in your family.

the grump meter ™

for kids and their families

Do you sometimes feel calm as the clear blue sky?

Well, the Grump Meter is for you,
for calm blue times and
red exploding times, for all the times you
are angry, and even
when you're not.

And do you sometimes feel like a volcano, ready to explode?

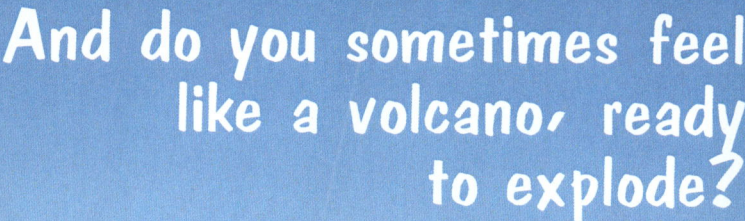

(This volcano could erupt at any time!)

What's the goal with the Grump Meter?

Stay on blue.

Prevent the trip to red.

And when you start to go

up the Grump Meter,

find a way to come back down!

blue

Sometimes you feel peaceful as a bird
soaring in the sky,
calm as the water on a lake at dawn.

When you're on blue,
do you notice if you're steady?
Ready for anything that comes your way?

Do thoughts pass through your mind calmly?
Does your voice sound cheerful or relaxed?
Is your breathing slow and even?
Are you able to do what you're asked?

green

On green you feel, well, a little GRUMPY.

How does your body feel?
How's your breathing?
How's your heartbeat?
Are your thoughts starting to rush?
Do you feel a little frustrated or crushed?

Are you starting to get hooked like a fish?

What's happened to take you to green?
What's changed inside of you?
What's changed outside of you?

Wasn't blue nice?

yellow

Slow down! Look around.

Is your heart beating faster?

Are your thoughts
speeding up?

Do you feel tense or shaky?

Do you need an out?
Do you need a thinking time-out?

On the road, a yellow light means
"slow down!"
Can you slow down?
Can you back up?
Back down?

It's not too late yet.

Be careful...

Are you on your way up, rolling up to orange?

Orange

Is your temperature going up?
Do you feel the heat of anger?
Is your breathing even faster?
Are your angry thoughts taking over?
Are you screaming or yelling?
Are you ready to hurt someone else
Or yourself?

Or can you think new thoughts to cool off?

It's still not too late. Orange is your last stop
before climbing to red.
You have a last chance to come back down
the Grump Meter.

Can you do it?
Can you talk yourself down?
Can you still make a choice?

Can you step on the brake?

Step on the brake!

red

Oh, no!
Did you forget to stop
on orange?
You landed on red!

Has the fire spread?
Have you blown your top?
Burst your balloon?
Lost control?
Said dangerous words?
Have you hurt anything or anybody?
Bullied somebody?
Have you hurt yourself?

How is your breathing? Your voice?
What are your hands doing?
How is your body moving?
What are your thoughts telling you?

Explode

You landed on red.
Oh no!

You've always got

Go back to
blue.

another chance.

**Start
on blue
again.**

Let's Make a Grump Meter

Design your own Grump Meter. It can be any size. It can be small to travel with, or big to hang on a bedroom door. Everyone in your family can make one and use it. Hang one on the fridge. Have a wall of Grump Meter art in the kitchen. Just make sure that the colors go from top to bottom in this order:

Red
Orange
Yellow
Green
Blue

Carry a Grump Meter everywhere—on your backpack, bike, or scooter.

The Grump Meter can help everyone in your family manage anger and have more calm. Everyone can make a Grump Meter. Everyone gets to prevent upsetting behavior. Everyone gets to participate.

Kids using the Grump Meter have made these comments about it. See what you could add to this list of thoughts.

Teenagers have said:

Identifying my mood will always come in handy—no matter where I live, or how I act, or what my behaviors look like.

When I look at the Grump Meter, I snap back into reality—I see that I need to control myself.

The Grump Meter is one of my main coping skills.

I lived in the orange all day but never went up to red.

I reminded myself to stay on blue and green.

It's great to know your mind is alert. You have options and choices if you are thinking for yourself.

When you're on the verge of doing something unsafe, that's an urge. When you have the Grump Meter in front of you, you can stop yourself from taking action on that urge. You have something to think about and consider.

Knowing you can have control of yourself is a great feeling.

We can draw it and draw it to make it our very own.

With the Grump Meter, you have an open mind. There's room for cognitive thinking. You are able to look beyond your anger. You can think of a new choice.

It's a fun tool. I smile when I use it!

Children have said:

The Grump Meter is fun—it's becoming part of me.

Stay on blue.

Think about the next color.

Think about what's happening to you.

Stay away from red.

Put your foot on the brake.

I can do it. I can get back down.

I'm going to have a blue day.

I stayed on blue all day.

Yeah!

Your Comments?

FOR PARENTS, GRANDPARENTS, TEACHERS & FRIENDS

Join in!

Point to the Grump Meter.
Pick your color.
Name your mood and feeling.
Take a time out.
Find your way back to yellow, green, and blue.

INTRODUCTION
THE EVOLUTION OF THE GRUMP METER

Like a compass on a long hike, the Grump Meter offers a tool for the journey that we humans travel many times a day. The journey takes us up the meter and down, then up and down again. We live with changes in our moods throughout our days, but there is the possibility of avoiding the extremes of emotional outbursts and staying in the middle of the climb, to modulate and mediate our angry responses and actions.

The Grump Meter works, but not by itself. It needs parents, kids, and sometimes caregivers and teachers to use it. Using it means keeping our eyes on it and on each other. It means finding words to talk about what's going on with our upset and angry moods and behavior. It involves finding new and creative responses to prevent and decrease destructive outbursts.

Kids use the Grump Meter in so many ways. They tell each other about it, teach each other how to use it, and teach their families. Kids even tell the judges in their court hearings that they're learning anger control with the Grump Meter.

People are glad to have new avenues for talking about anger and feelings in their families, and grateful for the possibility that everyone really can safely express and control their anger. Parents smile when they see it. Using the Grump Meter with families, we constantly discover new kinds of conversations to have, new words to use. As you use the Grump Meter, bring your own insight and ask your own questions with your children. The Grump Meter works as we work with it.

In this book, we focus specifically on the spectrum of feeling from calm to angry, and the associated temper tantrums, bullying, and outbursts that happen when kids' anger gets out of control. The Grump Meter, with its bright colors, is a powerful visual aid and has led us to rich discussion and exploration with young people. Because kids react so immediately and positively to the colors, the Grump Meter offers a start to working with anger; it goes a long way toward helping us negotiate and manage the expression of feeling in new ways. Kids have fun making their own Grump Meters and have found meaning in their own artistic expression. They make quick associations between the colors and their feelings. They find the language of color easy to remember and easy to teach their families and peers.

The Grump Meter colors, going from blue up to red are in contrast to the colors typically associated with the spectrum of emotion going from sadness to joy. On that spectrum, yellow and orange are typically associated with bright, sunshine-y feelings, and people sing "the blues" when they're down and depressed (cause your baby left you and the dog died). Surely the feelings on the "blues" spectrum are connected to the feelings on the anger spectrum; fear, insecurity, depression, and other feelings we associate with "the blues" can lead to anger or be the flipped side of it. But for the purposes of helping children reign in out-of-control, self-destructive, and destructive behavior, we focus purposely here on the rise from calm blue to explosive red. Keep returning to the kids' section of this book to clarify the associations between the calm of blue and the out-of-control of red.

Throughout this book, we speak in an editorial "we," but below we introduce ourselves to you and tell you about how we came to this project from Lynn's perspective as a social worker, and Janet's perspective as a parent and teacher.

Lynn Kaufman

When I began working in a residential treatment center with young people who couldn't control their behavior, I basically signed-on-the-dotted-line that I would teach anger control to all ages of kids all the time. This seemed like a great project. Anger without alternatives, reasonable means of expression, and limits, causes monstrous problems. I witnessed those problems first hand. The kids' anger flew, sparked, and spread like forest fires. And once the cycle of anger began, it had to burn itself out. Nothing could stop it in the middle.

Over many years, I have seen how children and teens with anger control problems can become destructive to themselves and others. With statistics telling us that eighteen children a day die from suicide, and so many others engage in self-harm and bullying, we need to pay attention to children's anger from the earliest moments of their lives. Anger doesn't go away or get better by itself. Children need coaching to learn to manage it.

Seeing the damage that uncontrolled anger does to kids and families, I have come to three conclusions:

1. It's helpful to kids and families alike to have a tool to address anger.

2. Kids and their family members need to be aware of the feelings that spark their rage and its accompanying behavior. Helping kids involves helping their families acknowledge anger, frustration, and fear connected to aggressive behavior.

3. Kids' big explosions have to be prevented. Kids having trouble expressing their anger appropriately need to notice and articulate their feelings, instead of acting them out. We see this happen with kids daily, in our households, on playgrounds, and in classrooms. As the poet Muriel Rukeyser recognized, our internal wars can become outward violence.

So, with inspiration from a friend, I devised the Grump Meter. Colorful and kid-friendly, and not threatening, the Grump Meter makes sense to kids. It gives them a vocabulary to name and describe their angry moods. And it gives them a frame of reference not only outside themselves as the Grump Meter hangs on the wall, but also inside themselves; they become able to internally visualize their climb from blue to red, refer to the colors in their own minds, and manage their anger in new ways.

All kids can make their own Grump Meters, and Grump Meters can hang everywhere—in bedrooms, doorways, halls, stairways, on bathroom doors, office doors, kitchen appliances, and anywhere with an open space. Kids can be reminded to use the Grump Meter wherever they are.

JANET KAUFMAN

As a parent, I am always seeking tools to help my children grow and learn. Parenting requires a kind of imagination, determination, and cleverness that seems beyond our grasp at times, and having a tool to de-escalate anger, and bring equanimity and peace into our family is vital. Together we keep finding new ways to use the Grump Meter as we change and grow, and as new behaviors and stages of development manifest themselves in our family. Some of the approaches to using the Grump Meter that we describe in this book come directly from our own experiments with it.

Through my experiences of reading with my children, I came to teach children's literature at the university. In doing so, I found myself exploring child development in new ways, and studying about how children learn to grow as emotional beings. Reading children's literature has clarified to me that we, as parents, need to help children see their own lives as vividly as Maurice Sendak shows us Max seeing himself among the wild things. We need to help our children see their frustration, anger, and behavior with such awareness that they can grow up learning to be in control and in charge of themselves. It is a hard task to help a child see him or herself, when we, ourselves, do not always know what we are looking at, and when our own feelings and reactions get in the way. So the Grump Meter is a tool to help everyone in the family sustain calm and prevent anger from getting out of control.

As Newton taught us with the law of gravity, and as the old Blood, Sweat, and Tears song goes, "What goes up, must come down." If we go up the Grump Meter, we have to come down. The higher we go, the harder it is to come down, and the more damage we are likely to do to ourselves or others. We do not need to take kids' anger away—as parents, we can affirm to our children that we all have a right to our angry feelings. But we can help them learn to express their anger safely. So the goal is to stay on blue, green, or yellow. Then we don't have so far to come down.

Practical Approaches To Using The Grump Meter

Here we offer some specific ways to use the Grump Meter. Consider this list a beginning, and add your own ideas to it. The goal of these approaches is to spur thinking and reflection that leads children to be able to control their behavior in positive ways.

Remember that using the Grump Meter, and controlling the expression of anger, is a family project. Thus each of the ideas below involves parents and children working together. Children and teens need their parents' involvement and guidance to becoming more aware of and identify their feelings. The model of their parents paying attention and bringing awareness to feelings accelerates children's ability to grow.

1. **Designing a Grump Meter:** Have your child design a Grump Meter, or everyone in the family can make one as a family project (see page 16). The conversation about anger control starts here. Say to your children or family, "Let's make a Grump Meter. We'll use it to help us manage anger with good will and humor in our family. All you need is magic markers and cardboard (or a piece of paper). Let's get started." Your Grump Meters can be very basic

or have a fun shape, like examples in this book. Jonah made one with little question marks written all around it. When asked why he added the question marks, he replied, "Because I want to ask what each color means." And then he added, "The question marks say, "What color are you on?"

2. **Pointing to the Grump Meter:** When you first start working with the Grump Meter, ask your child to point to his or her color every hour or two. Doing this when your child is in a calm, good mood might seem pointless, but that's precisely the time to do it. In a good mood, the Grump Meter can be fun and easy. You will help your child notice his or her calm moods and distinguish different emotional states. Remember, too, that practice is important. If a child is not used to using the Grump Meter when calm, then doing it in the middle of a temper tantrum won't work at all.

3. **Brainstorming:** While you and your child are both on blue and have time, brainstorm ideas about how to come back down the Grump Meter once you've gone up. Do this when you're both relaxed and have time. Write down the ideas your child has so that he knows you are taking him seriously, and offer some of your own. These might include having a snack, sipping a cup of tea or hot chocolate, spending some quiet time in your room, going outside to get some fresh air, reading alone or together, drawing, listening to music, or taking deep breaths.

4. **No Bribing:** Keep the Grump Meter strategies separate from rewards. If a child escalates to orange, she should not get to invite a friend over as a way to calm down—she has to calm herself down and show that she can stay calm. And do not let her confuse you by telling you, "If you wouldn't ask me to clean my room, I wouldn't go to orange or red!" Working with the Grump Meter helps us emphasize that it is not a parent's responsibility to calm a child down; instead, the parent can encourage the child to use the Grump Meter to be able to calm herself down.

5. **Staying Cool:** Think of the calming down or cooling time as learning and thinking time. With a young child, this may be time alone in the child's room or in the corner of the kitchen near the parent. The idea is not to punish, but to teach the child that he or she can take time away from a situation to calm down—and calming down helps us see things differently. With a young child, you can have crayons and paper ready for this time, which might also lead to valuable self-expression.

6. **Taking Thinking Time:** Take a "thinking time-out" with your child. For instance, set aside five or ten minutes with your child each day after school to review an incident, be it positive or negative. The incident could be something that happened at home or at school. Reflect with the child on how he reacted, what his internal and external triggers were, which color he rose to on the Grump Meter, how he brought himself back down (or failed to), and what other responses he could have given to the situation. Bring in

any visual aids you can think of in addition to the Grump Meter, such as the homemade stop sign we refer to in point #9 below. "Thinking time" conversation every day for a few weeks or longer gives the child focused, calm, meaningful attention with the parent. It also helps the child establish a routine of reflection, and begin to develop new patterns of thought and behavior.

7. **Using Grump Meter Language:** The moment you notice your child beginning to escalate emotionally, no matter how subtly, intervene with the language of the Grump Meter. Ask if she notices what color she's on. Ask her what she can do right now to come back to blue. Make sure she knows that she's the only one who can bring herself back down the Grump Meter. Don't escalate with her. Remember that your job is to stay in control to help your child learn.

8. **Finding Triggers—Outside and Inside:** Begin a conversation about outside and inside triggers that you can refer back to and develop over time. We discuss these triggers more fully on page 53, but basically, the outside trigger is an event that upsets us. It can be anything—a peer excluding a child on the playground, a parent commenting on a child's clothes, or a teen's romantic breakup. The inside triggers can be feelings of shame, fear, humiliation, and insult that are sparked by the outside trigger.

After an incident when your child has risen up the Grump Meter and has subsequently calmed down, you can begin a discussion about the scenario by asking what took him up the Grump Meter. Was he blaming an outside event for being upset or angry? Was he making difficulty or trouble where there was no tangible trouble? Was he bullying or causing trouble to another child? Was he unable to walk away from someone else's difficult behavior? Did he notice his frustration, anger, or fear building before he reacted? Keep the conversation going to help your child develop awareness. Bring up questions about inside and outside triggers when you and your child are both on blue, and ask your child if he'll commit to staying on blue while you talk together.

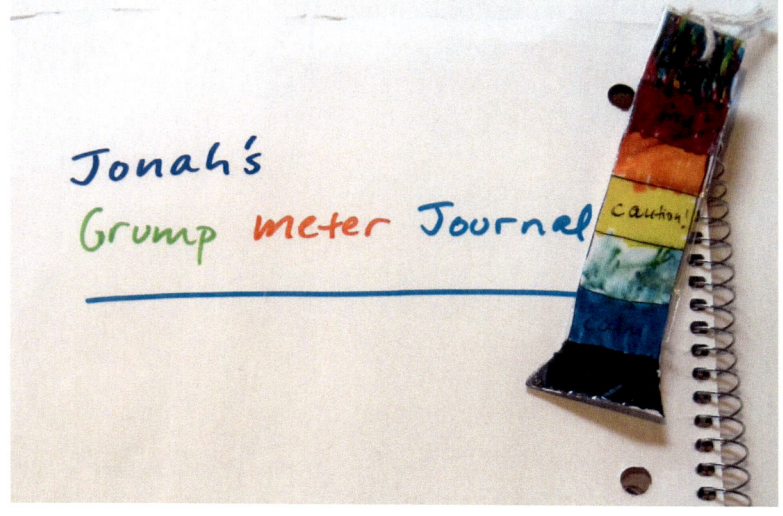

9. **Making a Grump Meter Journal:** Keep a "Grump Meter Journal" for children even as young as three. Use a slim spiral notebook and label the front "Grump Meter Journal."

Have your child make a Grump Meter, cover it with clear packing tape, put a hole through the top, and tie it to the spiral wire with a string.

When you start the journal, sit with your child and brainstorm ideas for writing and coloring that your child and you can do on different pages. If your child is young, you can write while he/she talks. For example:

- One page can hold the child's comments about how she feels when she's on each color.

- On another page, have your child draw a traffic light with yellow as the biggest circle. Remind her that on yellow, she can take "thinking time" to prevent going up the Grump Meter.

- In the journal, focus on safety and safe behavior. Have the child draw pictures or write about how he stays safe—wearing a helmet on his bike, looking both ways before crossing the street, keeping his hands to himself, etc. The idea here is to help  children remember that when they stay calm, they keep themselves and others safe—they don't hit, throw, or kick someone. Five-year old Jonah got inspired and made a series of stop signs to remind himself to stop before landing on red.

- On other pages of the Grump Meter Journal, make a chart to help your child track his anger and mood control. Write the date at the top of each page. Write times of the day down the left column—10:30am,

12:30pm, 2:30pm, etc. Then, on the rows, the child can draw the Grump Meter color he is on.

The Grump Meter journal can accompany your child to school. Get your child's teacher involved in the project to support the effort and ensure follow-through. The journal can help a teacher team with parents for consistency and offers the teacher a tool to create more structure for children. After a couple weeks of working with the Grump Meter journal and charting his colors routinely during the school day, Jonah piped up on the way to kindergarten, "I'm going to have a blue day." He anticipated how his day would go, and showed awareness that he could be in control of his behavior. Using the

Grump Meter offers constancy, confidence, habit formation, and ongoing conversation that results in steady behavior change.

10. **Working Together**: Parents, talk about the color you're on. Kids, talk about the color you're on. Together, figure out how to stay away from red and get back down to yellow, green, and blue. You can take quiet time, away time, or thinking time to calm down and cool off. Then start talking again when everyone is back on blue. For staying on blue, green, or yellow and taking "thinking time-outs," spend time together doing something special together.

Practice these approaches, and find your own ways to use the Grump Meter.

USING THE GRUMP METER:
FOUR DISTINCT TASKS TO KEEP IN MIND

As you see with the ideas above, you can work with the Grump Meter in many ways and situations. Below we distinguish four basic tasks to keep in mind with any approach you take.

TASK #1: TRACKING FEELINGS—A FAMILY MATTER

Use the Grump Meter as a family tool. Parents' awareness, attention, the light they can shed on a situation, and their faith in their children to grow is where the work of the Grump Meter begins. When we can help children track their feelings, we've taken a huge step forward in helping them control their behavior. When they can name the color they're on, they can also stop, think, talk, take the time to back up, and go back down to green and blue.

Creating awareness is powerful. In one family, three-year old David saw his big sister using the Grump Meter and asked to use it also. His mother doubted he was old enough to understand the significance of the colors, but the next time he was heading toward a temper tantrum, she interrupted him to ask what color he was on. "Green," he replied. Immediately, startled into recognition, he calmed down. To calm down, we need to realize:

1. We have different emotional states and feelings.
2. We can be aware of those states and feelings.
3. We can use tools to control the expression of our feelings.

Whether we're talking about young children having normal temper tantrums, school aged children acting impulsively on the playground, teens bullying each other, or kids suffering from trauma, young people have too little awareness of their own feelings. Having them notice when they are calm helps. Let the Grump Meter become an important part of them. For this to happen, they have to use it regularly.

Sometimes children and teens live in the orange. They stay close to red, close to exploding. Rarely in the blue and green, they hardly get a break from their anger. Imagine the teenager Lynn worked with who sneaked a bottle of nail polish in the morning, held onto it all day, waited until evening to break it, and intentionally cut herself using the glass. She seemed to have stayed stuck on Grump Meter orange all day, apparently not recognizing or distinguishing her escalated level of feeling, which seemed normal to her. No one had asked her all day how she felt. No one had asked her to point to the Grump Meter, though there was one hanging on the wall. In other words, no one helped her recognize her feelings, or noticed her sustained rage. Certainly, had she been asked to point to the Grump Meter, she could have been dishonest about the color she was on. But she wasn't given a chance. The adults around her missed her escalation, and she ended up hurting herself. After the fact, when Lynn did ask her if she'd been stuck in orange all day, she acknowledged that in fact she had been very angry.

This story highlights a major point: Kids often can't be left to notice their feelings on their own. Adults need to help their children check in with their own feelings. Kids need the grownups in their lives to pay attention, know when they're escalating, and care to help them. And kids want to know that the grownups are using the Grump Meter, too, to work on and control their own anger.

Helping kids at any age connect their feelings and behavior to colors on the Grump Meter can help them make mental and emotional distinctions, and thus help them make choices on the side of helpful and healing behavior. Even very young children can learn to recognize colors, attach them to feelings, and control themselves. They must do this if they are to grow to be emotionally healthy and live well with others in families, at work, and in play.

Help kids notice the color they're on!

Task #2: Preventing the Climb to Red— Paying Attention to Yellow

Make the Grump Meter very simple: Help each child pay attention to arrival on yellow. While you're grumpy on green, at yellow you've gotten to the halfway mark between blue and red. If children can recognize when they're on yellow, they can take their own calming down time or thinking time-out to lower their internal temperature. Time-out and thinking time offer an opportunity for children or teens to take themselves safely away from a difficult scene so they can calm themselves down and see new solutions to old problems. Parents can do this too—note when you're on yellow and need a thinking time-out so that you don't escalate. Paying attention to yellow can prevent you from going to red.

Here are some ways to express anger safely on green or yellow that can keep us from rising to red:

- Be honest. Say you're angry.
- State the reason you're angry and who you're angry at.
- Speak with an angry tone of voice. You can even yell.
- Make angry expressions with your face.
- Write your angry thoughts.
- Write a letter to the person you're angry at.
- Punch a punching bag.

Pay attention to yellow!

Task #3: Reminders
Finding Your Way Back Down

Children going to red will face consequences. It is up to the parent to decide what the appropriate consequences will be of repeated rides to red; a child might miss a game night, a movie night, or an ice cream out.

The late psychologist Arnold Goldstein used the term "reminders" to describe a practical strategy in anger management. Reminders are self-talk or cues that can be used to remind us to calm down in a tough moment so that we do not end up facing consequences. The reminders can be as simple as the child saying to himself: "Don't go to red or I'll miss family game night."

You can help your child make efforts to avoid red by discussing the reminders ahead of time. Let your child know in advance that there will be consequences for going to red. Then plan and discuss in advance how he or she will handle angry moments that build on each other, and how reminders would help. The name of the game is prevention.

With help, even children as young as three can brainstorm a list of ways to calm themselves down. Kids do need a plan for what to do when they start climbing the Grump Meter, and "reminders" are a tool to help carry out the plan. An adult collaborating with them is helpful. Don't wait for your child to escalate to figure out what to do.

Remember: If you don't remind yourself to calm down, you risk going to red and facing a consequence.

TASK #4: HAVING FUN!

Have fun! Be playful. Kids like the Grump Meter because it adds humor to their situations. By helping them see their anger more objectively, the Grump Meter makes it more manageable. The whole family has a chance to see anger with more distance and lightness. As children learn anger control and the skills that go with it, they feel accomplished ("I had a blue day, Mom!") and can have a sense of humor about their feelings. And they become empowered to teach others—to tell them how it's done and share their own accomplishments.

Points to Remember
for Regulating Emotional States

Regulating emotional states means that we can recognize when we're calm and we can stay calm, or we can recognize when we're upset and find a way to calm down. Here are four main points to remember when using the Grump Meter.

1. Recognize how you feel and where you are on the Grump Meter at any given time. Think of it as a map: You know where you want to go, but you have to identify your current location to figure out the best route to your destination. Knowing where you are on the Grump Meter can help you choose and control where you're going.

2. To prevent a quick climb to red, get thoughts and feelings working in tandem with your behavior. If you forget to pay attention to the colors, it's too late—you enter a zone of no self-control, and your anger controls you instead of you controlling it. That anger brings us to a dark place. To illustrate this with kids, Lynn switches off the lights and has everyone sit in darkness. The room becomes silent, still, and ominous: you cannot see yourself in the dark. Kids get it.

3. Know all five colors of the Grump Meter inside yourself. Just knowing when we're rising to red isn't enough. When we know what it feels like to be on each color, we can help ourselves stay on blue and green, or get ourselves back to blue when we need to.

4. Check in with the Grump Meter on a regular basis. Use the Grump Meter in the course of daily conversation, at any time of day, in any given moment—when kids are getting ready for school, eating breakfast, or playing a game. Ask, "What color are you on?... What happened that took you from blue to yellow just now?" or "What helped you come back down from yellow to blue?" Keep teaching your children. Do anything you can to create awareness.

It has been striking to witness how a simple tool, used with a good deal of conversation, intention, and much practice and follow-through, can help kids begin to understand themselves better and become empowered to control themselves and find calmer, more content ways of being in the world.

THINKING TIME
A DIALOGUE BETWEEN A PARENT AND SON, AGE 5

In the dialogue below, you see a parent and Steven, a five-year-old son, interacting in one of their daily "thinking times" after a troubling playground incident. Notice how the parent introduces the idea of internal and external triggers in this conversation, and reviews the incident step-by-step to help Steven reflect on the connection between his feelings and action. You'll see that the boy's ability to reflect verbally in the moment is limited, but the parent keeps the conversation going to emphasize the importance of verbal reflection, and to give the boy new ways of seeing.

Parent: Your teacher told me after school that you hit Colin on the playground today. What happened?

Steven: Well, Colin told me I couldn't go down the slide and that wasn't fair. So I got mad.

Parent: That's what we call an outside trigger—something that happens outside of you, which leads to you feeling upset inside. Did you rise to red on the Grump Meter in a flash? What were you thinking or feeling just before you hit Colin?

Steven: I don't know. I just got mad.

Parent: It sounds like you felt Colin wasn't being fair and excluding you—leaving you out.

Steven: Yeah, Colin was leaving me out and that wasn't nice. I didn't want to be left out.

Parent: It's very upsetting to be left out. None of us likes it. Feeling left out sounds like the inside trigger—the feeling inside you that felt so strongly when you hit Colin.

Steven: Yeah, he had no right to say that to me.

Parent: Well, no matter what Colin did, you have to pay attention to your own behavior, because hitting is not ok. Did you feel your breath changing when Colin told you not to go down the slide? Did you feel your thoughts getting faster? Did you notice you were getting very angry?

Steven: No. I just got angry. It just happened. I don't remember what I was thinking. My hand just shot out at Colin.

Parent: Well, let's pretend we could slow down the action, like putting the scene in slow motion. If you had gone to green or yellow instead of red, what would the scene have looked like?

Steven: I would have said, "Colin, that's not fair and I'm leaving to play with someone else."

Parent: Great. What else could you have done if you had gone to green or yellow?

Steven: I could have said, "Colin, that's not fair and I'm going to get help from a grownup."

Parent: That's another great idea. Do you remember the stop signs we made the other day? Go get one.

(Steven leaves to go get one of his paper stop signs, then returns.)

Parent: OK, now hold it close to your face. When you start to get really mad, imagine you have the stop sign in front of you, and you can stop yourself before you get to red and hit someone. Let's practice: you be Colin and I'll be you.

A role-play ensues in which parent and son act out the scene a few different ways. Role-playing can help develop new patterns of behavior. After a few minutes of working at this, the parent concludes the thinking time session.

Parent: You've done great work today. Now you have another chance to do better on the playground tomorrow. Don't forget that stop sign.

When talking with even very young children, keep having confidence that they can learn to verbalize and respond to situations in new ways. You can take "thinking time" like this with a child every day to create new habits of reflection, and reinforce visual cues and reminders that will help a child respond differently to a rise of anger.

Use thinking time to reinforce new ways of thinking and behaving.

A Grump Meter Conversation
With Teens—Step by Step

The following conversation occurred with a group of twelve teens, ages 11-17, who were discussing the Grump Meter with Lynn in a group session. This conversation, like the one above, introduces the idea of "internal and external triggers"—inside feelings and outside events, and the relationship between the two. Following this dialogue, we explore the concept of the triggers in more depth.

The situation the teens discuss points to intense feelings of anger and humiliation, and the potential for harmful behavior. But notice how their discussion also shows their capacity to self-reflect, control and reduce harmful behavior, and find new possibilities for themselves. While the situation discussed in this conversation may seem different from those in your family, as you read, notice the way Jamie identifies her feelings—how she is able to use the colors to give language to her experience. Then notice how Lynn goes step-by-step with the kids, asking them to think about each comment made, and then asking a follow-up question. The goal is to help these young people bring awareness to the relationship between their feelings and their behavior.

Lynn: Let's look at the Grump Meter again. *(I put it in the middle of the table where everyone can see it.)* OK, I would like to know who could talk about rising to red this weekend and what the triggers were to get you there. Let's start when you were on blue and ok. Who is willing to take us through the steps it took to get to red, describe how it happened?

Jamie: I will. I started off on blue on Saturday morning—and then all of a sudden that afternoon, I was on red. I went from blue to red way too fast.

Lynn: Well, let's review the goal of using the Grump Meter.

Peer: The goal is to stop on each color and think where you are—don't let yourself get to red. Take a step back—slow down on yellow and think before your anger takes you to orange and then red.

Jamie: I forgot to slow down because I was too mad. I forgot to stop on yellow and think.

Lynn: What kind of thinking needs to happen on yellow?

Jamie: You can think about consequences or think about slowing down and taking a time out before you land on orange. Orange is too close to red! I did not stop at all—I was fine one minute and the next minute I went to red.

Lynn: So you recognize that you went from blue to red in a really big hurry. Tell us about the trigger that started your fast climb to red.

Jamie: One of the kids called me a racist black b---. I'm not racist. I am friends with lots of kids of different colors. But, I got sooo mad that I exploded and wanted to fight her.

Lynn: Is that the kind of bullying that gets you to red? What did you do?

Jamie: I didn't fight her—I poured my pop on her instead of hurting her.

Lynn: Good for you. Someone else might have exploded at bullying like that, but instead you let the pop explode. So you used some anger control. Actually, it sounds like you started going to red and then stopped on orange, before breaking the bottle or fighting. How did you feel when you were able to prevent yourself from going all the way to red?

Jamie: I felt better when I poured the pop, but I still wanted to fight.

Lynn: How long did you stay on orange? When did you leave it and go back to blue?

Jamie: Not till bedtime, and I poured the pop in the afternoon. I stayed mad all afternoon.

Lynn: So, the external trigger—the trigger outside of you—was the name the other person called you. "Racist black b----." Yes?

Jamie: Yeah. When she called me that I started burning up. I was steaming mad.

Lynn: All right, we established the external trigger. Now how do we understand the internal trigger—the inside trigger? How is it connected to the external trigger—the outside trigger?

Peer: Because you get so mad that your inside feelings get hooked.

Lynn: Yes, they sure do. Think of a fish getting hooked by a fishing rod. The external trigger hooks you and you feel the inside feelings—and off you go to red. What are the inside feelings that hook you?

Jamie: I was disrespected. I was insulted. I was hurt.

Peer: I can name some feelings that hook me—being ostracized, put down, feeling "less than," feeling embarrassed and shamed. Like you don't exist or you're left out—rejected, minimized—and you don't matter.

Lynn: It seems like disrespect, insult, and hurt are the key internal triggers. What other ideas do you have for understanding internal triggers?

Peer: Maybe the trigger brings up memories of some bad things you went through as a child. You remember pain, hurt, and trauma that made you feel "less than" somebody else, like when kids in school or your parents bullied you.

Lynn: How many of you have had those feelings from the internal trigger switch turning on? (All raise their hands.)Are there any other words for feelings that would take you up the ladder to red fast?

Peer: Yes—very personal insults and judgments. When I feel judged by someone else and their opinion doesn't fit me. My parents judged me and called me names. I felt very judged.

Peer: When I got spanked or hit or yelled at. Being hit starts me on the path to red.

Lynn: So, it sounds like when a family member acts aggressively toward you with words or actions, you rise to red pretty fast.

Peer: Yes, being hit or struck at home is the biggest insult. Even if I do something wrong or talk back, it is not necessary to spank a kid. When I think about my parents spanking me, I'm still angry.

Lynn: Of course you're angry. Hands are not for hitting. You're right. So... Why have this discussion? What can we learn from this discussion?

Peer: We want to develop skills to help us when we get triggered, and learn to stop before the internal trigger steps up the pace to red.

Peer: We can learn to identify an internal trigger so we can calm ourselves down, and learn to understand our own feelings and not just react to them. We can even learn to understand the pain of the internal trigger and refuse to go to red over someone else insulting us if we stop to think.

Lynn: Do you think this conversation will help you?

Peer: Yes, next time I think I can recognize the internal trigger—the feeling that I cannot cope with the insult. Then I won't pay attention to the insult so much.

Lynn: So you can pay attention to internal triggers and not be overtaken by them. You could separate them from the external triggers.

Peer: Yes, except when I am called "worthless" by my parents and called other names that do not fit me.

Peer: Yeah, I would go to red when I feel judged or labeled. I don't like labels. They're never right.

Lynn: Well, I hope this discussion allows you to recognize and identify the internal trigger and reduce its power over you. Other people throw words around like a ball. That does not mean that you have to catch the ball! Maybe you could drop the ball and let it go.

Awareness and change often happen slowly and need steady attention. Toward the end of this conversation, the peers acknowledge how hard it is to separate themselves from the incidents they perceive as painful. The young people in this group had all explored internal and external triggers in therapy and with their families, and they had all been well-trained in the Grump Meter, had made their own Grump Meters, and had been asked to use them daily. But when this situation occurred, a review helped. And just as Lynn came up with the metaphor of the ball right at the end of the conversation, you will probably come up with your own metaphors when you have similar discussions. You can compare the Grump Meter to a traffic light, a stop sign, a thermometer, a ladder, or a rainbow. Janet's son Jonah was studying magnets in school, and we came up with a metaphor about magnets: we can be drawn to trouble like two magnets are drawn to each other. Or, as two magnets can repel each other, we can repel trouble.

IDENTIFYING TRIGGERS

We are indebted to Arnold Goldstein, who specialized in treating aggression and teaching prosocial skills, for the terms of internal and external triggers. Think of an outside trigger as any external event that makes us mad or upsets us. The outside trigger could be an insult, name-calling, teasing about clothes, comments about something like a date or a first kiss, or someone bumping into us accidentally. Virtually any event at all, intentional or accidental, could become an outside trigger.

Inside, or internal triggers, involve feelings of shame, humiliation, fear, or rage that live inside us from earlier events and moments in our lives. Any external event can reignite these painful feelings and trigger a rise up the Grump Meter. It is our perception of the outside trigger that matters, not the event or trigger itself. Often we blame the external event for upsetting us, without realizing that it was not the event itself that caused our feeling, but the tender place inside us that it touched. That upset or hurt feeling inside leads us to blame the outside event for our anger.

For example, take Jessica, who is walking back to her class from lunch when Amy accidentally bumps into her, and Jessica trips. She hits Amy. In this case, the outside trigger is Amy bumping into Jessica. The inside trigger that the event sparks, as Jessica identifies it only later, is Jessica's deep-seated anger and shame from feeling picked on and tripped up by her family.

When kids are struggling with their behavior or have escalated, you can ask them specifically:

- What were your inside and outside triggers?
- How important was the outside trigger?
- What did the trigger mean to you?
- How did the trigger get to be so important that it could spike your behavior up to orange or red?
- How did the trigger overpower any other choices you could have made?

Adults experience inside and outside triggers also. Parents, use yellow as your own caution light. It's not hard to get frustrated and angry oneself as a parent. Before spanking or hitting a child for their behavior that is sending you to red, stay on yellow and detour to "thinking time." Decide whether spanking or hitting is the best intervention for changing the child's behavior. Physical aggression toward a child can create pathways to problems in the child's future, including mental health concerns, parent-child conflict, and eventual aggression in children's behavior. Identifying and understanding our own triggers can help lead us to peaceful interventions with our children.

The Grump Meter as a Visual Aid

Having the visual image of the Grump Meter in front of them helps kids as they work on aligning their behavior with newfound insight about their feelings. After a while, they internalize the colors to help themselves de-escalate their reactions to anger, frustration, shame, and fear.

When kids have any kind of emotional hurt or a history of trauma, using the Grump Meter with exploratory conversation helps them distinguish between the outside and inside triggers. The visual aid of the five colors helps people of all ages see connections among their thoughts, feelings, and actions. As they make these connections, they learn to see the difference between the outer event and their inner perception of the event that reignited feelings of shame, humiliation, anger, and fear. Talking about triggers this way helps them identify the underlying deep "inside" feelings that can raise their internal temperature to boiling mad. Teasing out their sources of rage, shame, and secret struggles, children and teens alike can create new awareness about feelings from the past and situations in the present, and become better able to respond to what's happening in the present.

CURIOUS CONVERSATION
DISCOVERING THE STORY BEHIND ANGER

As in the dialogue above with the teens, when using the Grump Meter, we must talk about underlying experiences and feelings that lead to escalating behavior. Children and teens who have suffered from real or perceived trauma desperately need to learn about the feelings that trigger their aggressive behaviors. So always, we must address the sources of kids' anger. The sources of their anger are in their life stories. When we help them attend to the thoughts, feelings, and meanings they hold about their stories, they can see the connections between their behavior and their stories. They can begin to manage themselves in new ways. We like to think of the conversation we can have with kids about their upset feelings as "curious conversation," in which we inquire and discover together, learn about each other, and give kids room to voice their feelings. Through this conversation, kids can learn to put language to the inside and outside triggers that lead to their rise in anger and their outbursts.

WHERE DOES THE STORY COME FROM?

Kids' anger can come from situations that parents may or may not know about. Likewise, parents may know about certain traumatic situations but not realize they loom so large for their children. When young people's behavior is escalating severely and frequently, enough to cause damage to themselves or others, they may be suffering emotional pain from divorce, adoption, school problems, bullying, or other significant events, or have suffered physical or sexual aggression. These situations may not have been acknowledged in the family or may have remained unknown.

Sometimes, spanking or hitting kids can later lead them to extreme expressions of anger when they are older—fighting, cutting oneself, hurting others, hurting property, or attempting suicide. If young people reach this level of anger, they can be diagnosed with mental illnesses and treated medically. However, they may not be given the opportunity to describe their experiences and what is making them so angry. It is important to ask children what happened to them. Given the opportunity, people will discover their stories.

If we tried to tackle children's behavior alone without addressing their inner lives and ours, we would risk putting out the flames of the fire while leaving the embers burning. So dialogue within the family and sometimes with a therapist or someone outside the family can be vital to the work with the Grump Meter. Focusing on young people's stories gives us a way in to conversation that helps kids heal, and helps them begin matching their thoughts and feelings to their behavior.

A NOTE ABOUT PSYCHOTROPIC MEDICATION

When kids begin to understand their feelings through "curious conversation," training, and coaching, they begin feeling empowered to control their moods and, ultimately, their behaviors. At that time, they often express the desire to come off psychiatric medications they have been taking. They begin to feel the medications are no longer necessary to control themselves.

In recent years, parents have been worried about the long-term effects of these medications on their children, and question their efficacy and necessity. Parents often do not see that the medicines are making a difference and complain loudly about the quantity of medicines entering their children's bodies at such young ages. Both children and parents are articulating their concerns and challenging doctors more about these medications. Some physicians, however, too, are troubled by the use of these drugs. Dr. Mark Olfson, a Columbia University professor of clinical psychiatry, was quoted in The New York Times as saying, in response to a study he led about the treatment of antipsychotic drugs in young children, "There are too many children getting on too many of these drugs too soon."

In the population of children who have worked to understand and gain control of their feelings and develop self-management skills, many request being taken off the medications. It seems remarkable, indeed, that kids who may have been diagnosed with mental illness and treated with multiple strong medications can begin to manage well with peers and family. They can find language to put to their feelings and, in turn, become able to change and reorganize their behavior. They find new ways to express their need to be involved in their own lives and the lives of their families and friends.

A note about suicide

Given the rate of teen suicide in the United States, and the amount of self-harm and aggression seen in young people, it is clear that many children and teens at risk of harming others or themselves—by fighting, attacking, cutting themselves, and attempting suicide—live with tremendous shame, fear, and ultimately, rage. In one of her newspaper columns, Ann Landers wrote a letter to teens saying, "If you are thinking about suicide, you are furious with somebody. You can be furious without killing yourself or thinking you need the punishment of death." We adults owe it to kids to help them address their anger and find tools to stop themselves from dangerous behavior before it is too late.

Writers such as James Murphy in *Coping with Teen Suicide* and Michael Miller in *Dare to Live* discuss the importance of learning to acknowledge and express anger in useful and healthful ways. Most importantly, the kids Lynn works with teach her that rage is a profound contributing factor to their thinking about, gesturing, and attempting suicide. They have acknowledged the role of anger and rage in distorting their thoughts, and in leading them to think that they do not matter enough to keep living.

Attempting suicide could be seen as akin to having a severe temper tantrum. In Grump Meter terms, kids in such a state of rage have taken the trip to red and don't know how to get back down. With focused teaching, learning, and conversation, kids can learn to recognize the feelings connected to suicide ideation as Grump Meter red, and learn and practice coming back down the Meter so they don't decide to die while they're on red. They can learn to distinguish transitory and painful, difficult, complex moments and feelings from permanent situations. Certainly death is not an answer to angry moments on red.

Teenagers have said to Lynn, "If I had not been on red, I would not have tried to kill myself." Our hope is that by using this tool and others, many more young people can develop new skills to express themselves through language and other safe means that strengthen their lives.

A Curious Conversation Between
a Parent and a Child, Age 13

Often, kids and adults escalate because we get ourselves into a difficult or challenging place, and may feel unheard, unnoticed, or misunderstood. The following conversation grapples with these kinds of feelings. It takes place between a mother and her thirteen-year-old daughter, Kate, and illustrates the need for unexpressed feelings to be put into words, not actions. Thinking it essential to have intentional time together and focused, "curious conversation," Kate's mom takes her out to talk over ice cream.

Mom: I'm concerned about your trips to red. They're happening a lot and they're hurting you and everyone around you. I don't see them solving any problems. I'm wondering how we could find new ways to help you stop on yellow before you get to orange and red.

Kate: You know what's taking me to orange and red! You care more about your new boyfriend than me. It used to be just you and me. Now it's not. You talk to him more than me. You leave me out of conversation.

Mom: This is painful to hear, because I've heard you say this before and I'm trying hard to listen and talk with you. But it seems like you continue to feel left out. Even when I try to include you in the conversation, you don't feel that. Can you tell me what it would take to make you feel included?

Kate: When you played a game with me last night and we laughed together, I felt included and comforted. You made me feel so much better.

Mom: I'm glad we had a fun evening, and I'm glad I could comfort you, but I don't always know when and how to do that in the middle of the day, in a family situation, when you get so upset. I wonder what kind of attention I could give you to help you avoid red, so you don't end up so upset.

Kate: I'm going to red so you'll notice me!

Mom: Kate, you don't have to go to red to get noticed. I can notice you on blue, green, yellow, and even orange. I notice you every minute I am with you, and think about you constantly, and always love you. Sometimes I fail to notice what you want me to notice. But then you have to tell me. Please don't hurt yourself by going up to red and behaving badly so that I will notice you. You never have to do that. Maybe when you start going up the Grump Meter, we both need to stop and notice each other, and listen and talk to each other. I need you to tell me a signal to look for so I can know when you want to be noticed. I'll try very hard to look for those cues.

This is a "curious conversation." The mother remains curious, and the child discusses the initial question in response to the mom's curiosity, not her criticism. By expressing genuine curiosity about her daughter, the mom gives Kate a chance to express herself and make a connection between her behavior escalating and feeling unnoticed by her mother.

The discussion makes further work with the Grump Meter possible for both of them; by creating new awareness for herself and her mother, Kate has given her mother a new idea about how it might be helpful to respond. The conversation allows them both to keep distinguishing the external triggers from Kate's internal triggers of wanting to be noticed.

Continued curious conversation helps children break the habit of escalations. Finally, the conversation offers Kate an example and experience of finding comfort and being noticed by her mother through peaceful means. Children and teens hunger for such straightforward conversation to assure them they've been heard. There is healing in these conversations.

CLOSING WORDS
YOUNG PEOPLE COMMENT
ON THE USE OF THE GRUMP METER

Below you'll see comments written by children and teens, ages 10-18, after Lynn asked them to reflect on their use of the Grump Meter. The young people who wrote these words all had family members and a therapist working to help them manage their anger, grapple with their feelings, and control their behavior. The path that these kids took to describe their feelings of anger and control their disruptive behavior was not smooth. Yet, they have begun to develop a vocabulary for identifying feelings and reflecting on their behavior. Their comments speak to the possibility for young people to learn and change.

The Grump Meter makes you actually think about the levels of your anger. And it helps you calm down. It also helps you become a less angry person. And be more in control. Working with a Grump Meter helps me identify my levels of anger.

The Grump Meter helps you tell where your angry and upset moods are and how you feel them. The Grump Meter helps me level out my angry moods. When I get to orange, I've missed my thinking time. But that's better than going to red—I can take a time-out before I explode. You never want to get to red because that's when you know you've lost your cool.

The Grump Meter helps me identify my feelings. Self-talk to go back down helps.

I know I can stop before I get to red and start over on blue. The Grump Meter helps me keep myself, my friends, and my family safe.

Use the Grump Meter

Use the Grump Meter. It is a tool, not a picture on the wall. Use it frequently and consistently to let it become part of kids' emotional functioning. Have confidence that you can help children to express and manage their anger in ways that allow them to live well. And have confidence that kids can, indeed, learn and grow, no matter how difficult the challenges seem in the moment.

Have fun with the Grump Meter.

If you want to be in touch, ask us questions, or share stories, please visit us at www.GrumpMeter.com.

ACKNOWLEDGEMENTS

Over many years, we have collaborated professionally and personally as we have seen the intersections of Lynn's social work, Janet's teaching, and our lives together as mother, grandmother, and daughter. This book has evolved as an extension of ongoing conversation between us.

Innumerable friends, colleagues, clients, and students have inspired us, helped us, and continue to teach us:

Present and former colleagues and staff at KVC Behavioral Health Care have supported, enjoyed, and developed the work with the Grump Meter since 1990. Teaching anger control to out-of-control children and teens has been at the heart of KVC's residential program since its inception. It has been a privilege for Lynn to be part of the program and work with young people and families there.

In a casual conversation about children and parenting many years ago, Ellen Chilton used the term "grump meter," and planted a seed in Lynn's head that has continued to grow and matter over twenty years. We are indebted to her for a great idea.

Anya Baryshok has been our art coach, sitting with Rachel and Jonah, helping them hone their illustrations.

Dave Kreitzer captured the intention and spirit of this book to craft the design of it. We appreciate his diving into this project and bringing his thoughful care and artistic vision to it.

Suzanne Jeschke and Deborah Shouse read our manuscript with keen, caring eyes and helped us clarify and strengthen it.

So many children, teenagers, and parents have made good use of this tool for many years, and we thank those who have anonymously offered their words and pictures. Their thoughtfulness and generosity, their willingness to be open, their enthusiasm to grow, and their ability to find new ways to be aware of their feelings and thoughts, strengthens not only their lives, but also ours.

Many parents, friends, and mentors have offered questions and insights about the Grump Meter, and shared stories of their own struggles and experiences. Their enthusiasm for the Grump Meter and their appreciation of the need for this work has encouraged us.

Dan has offered his careful reading, finely-tuned insight and perspective, artistic ideas, and always, playfulness and love.

The unending technical support and support of so many other kinds from Andy, Dad, Saba has helped make this project, and so much in our lives, possible.

Writing this book has been a family journey for us, and we are grateful to Rachel and Jonah, and Sarah and Alex, for their inspiration, ideas, and art. As we worked, they gave us new ways of thinking about the Grump Meter, which in turn led to more drafting and revision, a genuine collaboration. Their responses to the Grump Meter and their artistic metaphors have given us important information within our own family, teaching us as we go. Their love brings joy to the journey. *Hazak, hazak, v'nithazek.* May you go from strength to strength, and may we strengthen each other.

fuming

exploding

boiling

raging

humiliated

betrayed

afraid

unloved

insulted

jealous

shamed

angry

left out

disappointed

let down

heard

open

content

important

calm

cared for